Beginning to END

Oil To Gas

A Buddy Book

by

Julie Murray

ABDO
Publishing Company

VISIT US AT
www.abdopublishing.com

Published by ABDO Publishing Company, 4940 Viking Drive, Edina, Minnesota 55435.

Copyright © 2007 by Abdo Consulting Group, Inc. International copyrights reserved in all countries. No part of this book may be reproduced in any form without written permission from the publisher. Buddy Books™ is a trademark and logo of ABDO Publishing Company.

Printed in the United States.

Coordinating Series Editor: Sarah Tieck
Contributing Editor: Michael P. Goecke
Graphic Design: Maria Hosley
Cover Photograph: Photos.com
Interior Photographs/Illustrations: David McNew/Getty Images (page 13), Media Bakery, Photos.com

Library of Congress Cataloging-in-Publication Data

Murray, Julie, 1969–
   Oil to gas / Julie Murray.
     p. cm. — (Beginning to end)
   Includes bibliographical references and index.
   ISBN-13: 978-1-59679-913-4
   ISBN-10: 1-59679-913-7
   1. Petroluem as fuel—Juvenile literature. 2. Gasoline—Juvenile literature. I. Title.

TP355.M87 2007
665.5'3827—dc22

2006019908

Table Of
Contents

Where Does Gas Come From?

Gas is an important **resource**. Many people need gas to **fuel** their cars. Gas also helps airplanes fly. And, gas provides energy to heat, cool, and light some people's homes.

Gas has many uses. Do you know where it comes from?

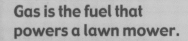

Gas is the fuel that powers a lawn mower.

A Starting
Point

Gas comes from oil. Oil comes from plant and animal **fossils**. This is why oil and gas are sometimes called fossil **fuels**.

Millions of years ago, plants and animals lived near the world's oceans. When they died, their remains settled to the ocean floor. Over time, these remains were buried beneath sand and **silt**. Because of heat and pressure, the remains turned into oil.

There are many layers of materials underground. Animal and plant remains are part of these layers. Sand and silt are, too.

Over time, scientists have learned how to find oil beneath rocks. Today, people drill deep into the Earth to get oil.

Sometimes workers build an oil well to dig on land. Other times they build oil wells to dig beneath the water. Oil can be found in many different places.

Some oil is found beneath the Earth's oceans.
There are special drills designed to get this oil.

Crude Oil

Gas comes from something called **crude** oil. Crude oil is a dark liquid with a strong smell. It is the raw form of oil.

Workers drill into the Earth to find crude oil. When they find crude oil, they build a well. The well pulls crude oil out of the Earth.

Oil wells help workers get crude oil out of the Earth.

11

FUN Facts
Did you know...

Lots of things are made of plastic.

Water Bottles   Glasses

... Many other products are made from oil. Plastic is one product made from oil.

Some toys are made of plastic, to

... **Crude** oil makes three types of **fuels** for transportation. These are propane, diesel, and gas.

Cars use gas.

Big trucks use diesel fuel.

4 million vehicles world-wide use propane.

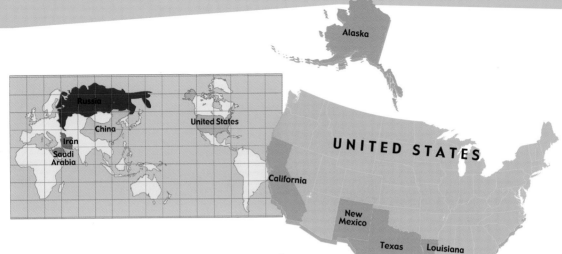

... The countries that produce the most oil are Saudi Arabia, Russia, the United States, Iran, and China. In the United States, the states that produce the most oil are Texas, Alaska, California, Louisiana, and New Mexico.

... Even though oil comes from the Earth, it can hurt plants and animals if it is spilled.

Oil was spilled in this bird's habitat. People will need to clean the oil from the bird's home and from its feathers in order for it to survive.

13

Refining Oil

In order for people to make **crude** oil into useful products, it must be **refined**. To do this, oil must be taken to a large **factory** called a refinery. Sometimes, barrels of oil are moved by ship or by truck. Other times oil is sent through a pipeline.

This ship is an oil tanker. It helps transport oil.

Just one barrel of **crude** oil can make many useful products. There are 42 gallons (159 L) of crude oil in one barrel. One thing it can be made into is gas. About 20 gallons (76 L) of gas can be made from each barrel.

But first, the oil must be **refined**. There are three important steps in refining crude oil. These are separation, conversion, and treatment.

42 Gallons of Crude Oil

20 Gallons of Gas

One barrel can hold 42 gallons (159 L) of crude oil. Those 42 gallons of crude can make about 20 gallons (76 L) of gas.

From Oil To Gas

Separation is the first step in **refining crude** oil. During separation, the oil travels through a special machine. This machine uses heat to separate the crude oil into different parts.

Next is conversion. Conversion is used to get as much gas as possible from the crude oil.

An oil refinery helps change oil into gas.

The last step is treatment. This process makes the gas ready for people to buy and use. After treatment, the gas is shipped to places around the world. Then, people buy the gas to **fuel** their cars and other vehicles.

The next time you ride in a car, think about how making gas from oil helps the car run.

Gas is the fuel that helps cars run.

Can You Guess?

Q: Oil is sometimes called petroleum. What does the word "petroleum" mean?

A: Rock oil.

Q: How is oil removed from the Earth?

A: By drilling.

Important Words

crude   something in a natural state.

factory   a business that uses machines to help with work.

fossil   the remains of plants and animals in the Earth.

fuel   a substance that provides energy.

refine   to remove parts that aren't wanted.

resource   a supply of something.

silt   very small particles that are smaller than sand, but larger than clay.

Web Sites

To learn more, visit ABDO Publishing Company on the World Wide Web. Web site links about this topic are featured on our Book Links page. These links are routinely monitored and updated to provide the most current information available.

www.abdopublishing.com

Index